a new light on STORM AT SEA QUILTS

ONE BLOCK—AN OCEAN OF DESIGN POSSIBILITIES

WENDY MATHSON

Text copyright © 2009 by Wendy Mathson

Artwork copyright © 2009 by C&T Publishing, Inc.

Publisher: AMY MARSON

Creative Director: GAILEN RUNGE

Editors: LISA E. RUBLE and KESEL WILSON

Technical Editors: CAROL ZENTGRAF and SANDY PETERSON

Copyeditor/Proofreader: WORDFIRM INC.

Cover Designer/Book Designer: KRISTEN YENCHE

Page Layout Artist: ROSE SHEIFER-WRIGHT

Production Coordinator: CASEY DUKES

Illustrator: WENDY MATHSON

Photography by CHRISTINA CARTY-FRANCIS and DIANE PEDERSEN of C&T Publishing unless otherwise noted

Published by C&T Publishing, Inc., P.O. Box 1456, Lafayette, CA 94549

Library of Congress Cataloging-in-Publication Data

Mathson, Wendy,

 A new light on storm at sea quilts / Wendy Mathson.

   p. cm.

 Summary: "An exploration of the design possibilities offered by the Storm at Sea quilt block, with 6 projects included"—Provided by publisher.

 ISBN 978-1-57120-578-0 (paper trade : alk. paper)

 1. Patchwork—Patterns. 2. Quilting—Patterns. I. Title.

 TT835M27369 2009

 746.46'041--dc22

                        2008025696

Printed in the USA

10 9 8 7 6 5 4

CONTENTS

INTRODUCTION TO STORM AT SEA

The pattern we know as the traditional Storm at Sea block has timeless appeal. The most striking aspect of the design is the suggestion of curves, even though it is pieced entirely with straight seams. There is a kind of universal attraction to this pattern—a fascination with the optical illusion of waves created with simple geometric shapes.

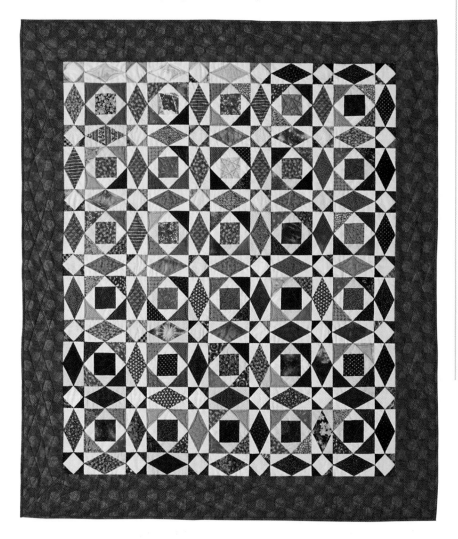

Any Blue Will Do, Faith Horsky.
Traditional-style Storm at Sea quilt

It is not hard to see where the pattern got its name. Can't you just see whitecaps on the choppy seas? This design has been a favorite with scrap quilters for many years, and it's no wonder that many older Storm at Sea quilts share a blue and white color scheme. The traditional pattern using alternating dark and light patches is just the tip of the iceberg on the stormy sea, however. This fascinating block provides almost endless design potential. Forget about just blue and white; what happens when you add color? How do medium-value fabrics change the pattern? What other illusions and patterns can be created with Storm at Sea units? This book is an exploration of the design possibilities and is meant to stimulate your creativity and show you how to create your own unique quilts.

you can piece this!

When I mention Storm at Sea to a quilter, the response I often hear is, "Oh, I've always wanted to make one of those…" And then, "…but they are so hard to piece!" The *typical* method of cutting patches with templates requires attention to detail and precision piecing. Sewing pieces with long, skinny points requires exact positioning of the patches for precise finished units. An alternative is paper foundation piecing, which produces accurate units but can be time-consuming and tedious—particularly the step of removing the paper.

This book introduces my *unique* piecing method: a fast, simple way to produce very accurate units using standard rotary-cutting techniques. The key to my method is a set of acrylic tools called Quilters' TRIMplates (short for trimming templates) available from C&T Publishing (see Resources, page 78).

- TRIMplates allow flexibility in piecing because the units are trimmed to size *after* sewing.

- As a unit is trimmed, it is easy to see that each seam and point falls exactly where it should.

- There are no more cut-off points, and no need to "fudge" the seam allowance when sewing units together.

- Cutting and piecing are faster because the patches are cut oversize and do not need to be precisely positioned.

- Finished units have the straight grain of the fabric on the outside edges, which makes it *much* easier to join the units together into a finished quilt.

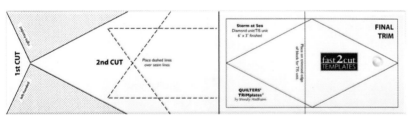

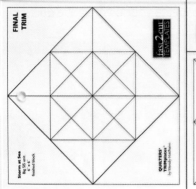
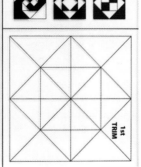

Quilters' TRIMplates

Of course, TRIMplates are not the only way to make Storm at Sea blocks, but a method that is simple, accurate, and enjoyable means we can make more quilts in less time. What a great way to explore the design possibilities of this versatile pattern!

how to use this book

Piecing with TRIMplates, page 25, explains how to use these tools, but I have also included foundation-paper-piecing template patterns, page 76, for those who prefer this method of piecing or who have not yet purchased the TRIMplates.

If you love to design your own quilts, *Exploring Design Possibilities*, page 6, walks you through the creative process and provides many examples as a starting point for your exploration. *What Else Can You Do with Storm at Sea?* page 14, expands on these ideas with more design options. The *Gallery*, page 36, should pique your interest in Storm at Sea even more.

When you are ready to begin sewing, choose your favorite piecing method and pick a project (beginning on page 53) or one of your own designs. The information and reference tables in *From Design to Fabric*, page 20, will help you plan your quilt and estimate yardage, as well as providing instructions and tips on piecing and quilt construction.

EXPLORING DESIGN POSSIBILITIES

analyzing the block

The traditional Storm at Sea design is made up of three pieced units: a rectangle, a large square, and a smaller square. The rectangle unit is easy to identify: it contains the Diamond shape. To distinguish the square units, I refer to them as "Big SIS" and "Little SIS." SIS is my shorthand for Square-in-a-Square.

Diamond unit   Big SIS   Little SIS
                     unit   unit

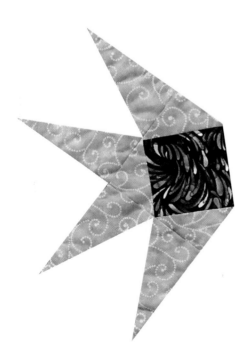

combining the units

Traditionally, these three units are arranged to make an allover repeating pattern. To understand how the units go together, think of a basic quilt set using blocks separated by sashing strips. A square cornerstone is pieced into the sashing strips where the vertical and horizontal strips intersect.

Cornerstone

Sashing

Sashing

Block

Basic quilt set

The standard Storm at Sea pattern is a series of Big SIS blocks joined together by pieced sashing and pieced cornerstones. The pieced sashing units are the Diamonds, and the cornerstones are Little SIS units.

Standard Storm at Sea set

There is another way to look at Storm at Sea. You can arrange one Big SIS, four Diamonds, and four Little SIS units into a single block. Sewing together multiple blocks like this results in a significantly different look. With this variation, two Diamond units appear side by side, and four Little SIS units come together to form a larger square. I call this the "double diamond" arrangement.

Double diamond arrangement

using the design grids

The best way to start exploring the potential of Storm at Sea is to play with the design grids, pages 74 and 75. Make multiple copies of the grids or simply use tracing paper positioned over a grid. Either way, get out your colored pencils and get ready to play. Some of you will readily see potential design elements: curves, stars, ribbons, hearts, and so on. I suggest you glance at the illustrations on the next few pages and then close the book and begin to color with the design grids.

For others, the designs will not be as easy to visualize. You might prefer to treat the next few pages as design exercises. Begin to shade in the grid using just one pencil color. Experiment by copying some of the illustrations until you begin to understand how the shapes relate to each other. Once you have worked out some of the designs on paper, it will be easier for you to move on to working with fabric.

TRADITIONAL DARK/LIGHT PATTERN

The basic Storm at Sea pattern uses alternating light and dark fabrics so each seam connects a light patch to a dark patch.

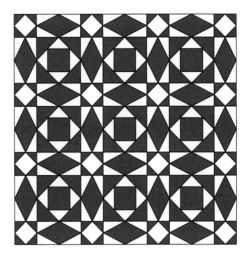

Traditional dark/light pattern

In the traditional dark/light Storm at Sea, the Diamonds are the dark fabrics. But what happens when you reverse the placement of lights and darks?

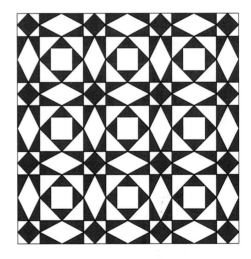

Reversed dark/light pattern

Notice that much more light fabric is used in this variation. Do you see stars popping out around each of the Little SIS units? One way to emphasize these stars is to reverse the dark/light placement only on the Little SIS units, as in the following diagram.

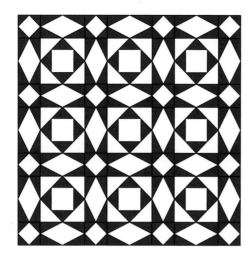

Dark stars

Of course, this variation can also be applied to the first pattern, the traditional dark/light version. Now the light stars seem to float against the dark background.

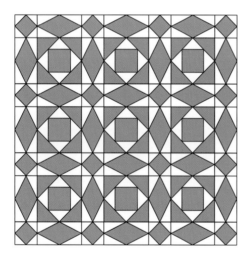

Light stars

So far, we have been using only the standard grid, page 74. Remember that we also have the double diamond grid, page 75, to play with. The simplest way to shade this version is to use darks and lights in the same patches in each block.

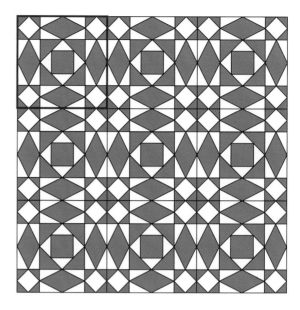

Dark/light on double diamond grid

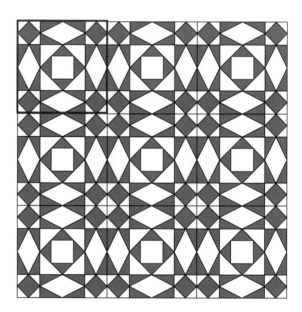

Reversed dark/light on double diamond grid

When the identical block is repeated in the double diamond grid, some light patches are sewn to light patches, and darks to darks.

What happens if we decide to go back to alternating dark and light patches? Where two Diamonds touch, one will be dark and the other light; the same shading carries into the Little SIS units. Now there are two different blocks, and one is the reverse of the other.

Dark/light variation on double diamond grid

At this point I hope you can see why the Storm at Sea pattern was a favorite of scrap quilters in the past. Using any of these pattern variations with high-contrast dark and light fabrics can result in a stunning quilt. But more magic occurs when you begin to play with value. By using light, medium, and dark fabrics and varying their placement, you can create any number of interesting effects that go far beyond the look of traditional Storm at Sea designs.

THE ILLUSION OF CURVES

Why do we see curves when we look at this pattern? The illusion comes as the eye connects the angled seams in the Diamond, Big SIS, and Little SIS units.

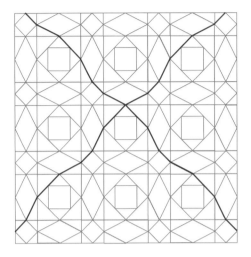

Standard grid

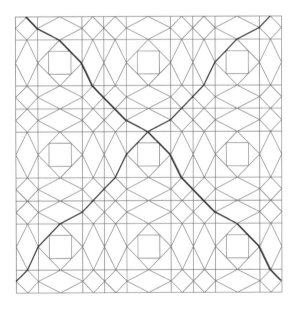

Double diamond grid

This effect can be accentuated by adding medium-value fabrics to connect the shapes into wavy ribbons.

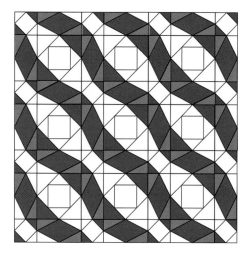

Ribbons on standard grid

If you reverse the dark/medium patches with the light patches, you get a very different wave effect. These waves look less like ribbons because they seem to get wider and narrower. The feeling of movement and the curves are still there, though.

Reversed ribbons on standard grid

Using the double diamond grid creates another ribbon effect altogether. Here the wavy ribbons and the wide/narrow waves seem to be combined.

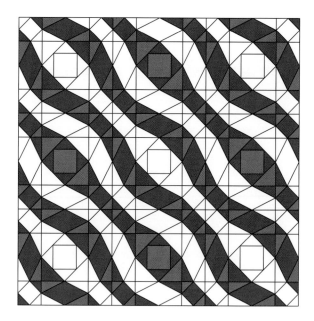

Ribbons on double diamond grid

You might have realized that the waves can run in two different directions. With a little manipulation, these ribbons can create wonderful interlocking and woven effects.

Waves in two directions

Waves in two directions with border

FINDING SHAPES IN THE GRIDS

Now we have something that is beginning to look more like an interesting quilt pattern! If you have been playing with the grids and your colored pencils, no doubt you have already begun to see even more possibilities using the standard grid. Can you find a heart? Do some of the shapes suggest flowers to you? We've already seen some stars. Have you found any other star designs? What happens when ribbons connect symmetrically to surround a star?

In case you have not already discovered these on your own, the next few pages are meant to be a starting point for your own design exercises. Try copying one or two of the patterns that appeal to you; then just do some doodling with your colored pencils to see what you can discover in the grids on your own. When you're ready to transform that paper design into fabric, see Estimating Yardage for Original Designs, page 21.

ALTERNATIVE WAYS TO CREATE ORIGINAL DESIGNS

If you've had enough of coloring in the design grids, try a different approach to design. You can cut a grid, page 74, into individual units and rearrange them to create any number of new and unique blocks and overall patterns. I suggest enlarging the grid by 200%–300% so your pieces are large enough to work with easily. For more stability, paste the enlarged grid onto card stock before cutting it apart.

Some of you would rather just jump into a pile of fabric and start sewing. Colored pencils and paper grids just aren't your style! An intuitive approach may suit you better than preplanning your entire piece. I suggest using a vertical design wall such as a foam insulation board covered with felt, flannel, or cotton batting. Simply cut a stack of the appropriate shapes in a variety of fabrics and begin to arrange them directly on the wall. I find it easier to work from the center and build outward, but this is a design method that just has no rules. You may prefer to sew some Diamond, Little SIS, and Big SIS units and then arrange them on the design wall until you get a feel for where your project is headed.

Standard grid (for blank grid, see page 74)

Double diamond grid (for blank grid, see page 75)

WHAT ELSE CAN YOU DO WITH STORM AT SEA?

border possibilities

Sometimes the addition of a pieced border can be the perfect finishing touch for a quilt. Storm at Sea borders have the advantage of providing a sense of motion and the suggestion of curves as an effective counterpoint to a geometrically pieced quilt. Of course, you don't need to limit yourself to putting Storm at Sea borders on Storm at Sea quilts.

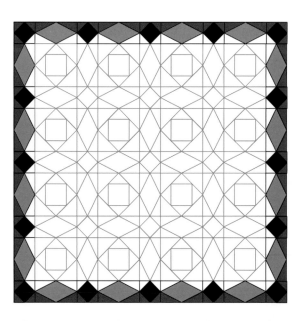

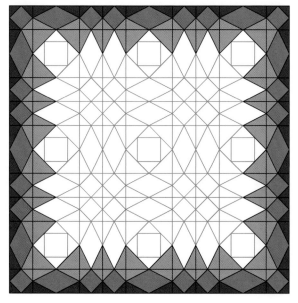

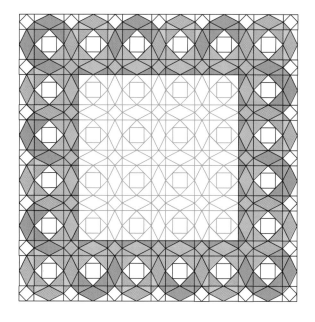

turning the grid on point

Another fascinating way to vary the look of any square design is to simply rotate it one quarter turn. This effectively puts the blocks on point. With the standard Storm at Sea dark/light shading, this seems to enhance the illusion of curves and gives a stronger feeling of movement in the piece.

Standard grid

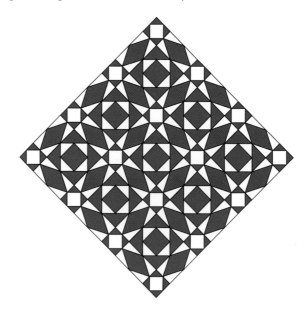

Standard grid on point

Double diamond grid

Double diamond grid on point

creating landscapes and pictorial quilts

Consider what happens when you use a grid on point as the framework for an overall quilt design. It is possible to create wonderful landscape and pictorial effects by delineating areas or rows of color.

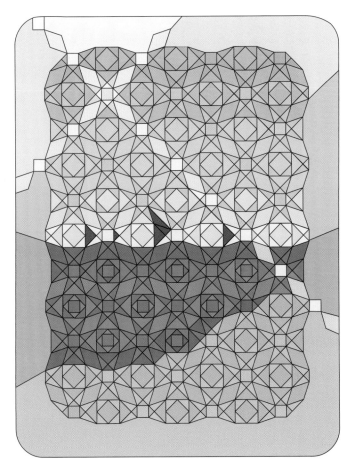

Smooth Sailing design by Wendy Mathson

The rotated grid provides new possibilities for isolating shapes, such as these intriguing interlocking hearts.

Interlocking Hearts design by Wendy Mathson

As exciting as these on-point quilts can be, the uneven edges that result can be a challenge for the novice quilter. If you are ready for a piecing challenge, you will have a great time using the grids in this manner. You can use bias binding to finish the undulating edges of the quilt or appliqué it to a background. A simpler solution is to piece a square design, then turn it 45° and sew large triangles on the corners to square it up again. *It Was a Dark and Stormy Night* and *Storm at Tiffany's Winery*, page 45, are examples of on-point quilts.

Even after several years of experimenting with Storm at Sea and teaching numerous workshops, I am continually amazed at the creativity displayed by my students. Just when I think I have seen almost every possible combination, someone comes up with something different and exciting. Following are two original designs by Linda Kamm.

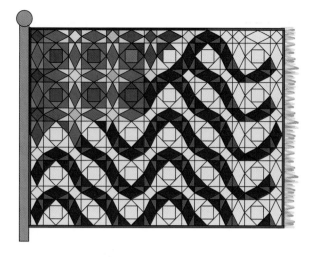

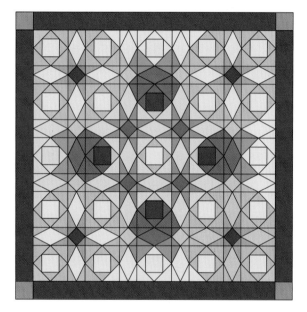

altering the grid

The next logical step is to consider subdividing patches into smaller shapes by adding lines to the grids. This is most easily accomplished with the two largest shapes: the Diamonds and the center square of the Big SIS.

CHANGING THE CENTER OF THE BIG SIS UNIT

Sometimes the large center of the Big SIS needs to be broken up into smaller pieces to give a better balance of color to the quilt. Try putting a four-patch in the center of the Big SIS, or, even better, replace the plain center square with a Little SIS unit, which just happens to be the same size.

Square center

Four-patch center

Little SIS center

BIG SIS VARIATIONS

Glance through the Gallery, pages 36–52, to get a sense of the sheer variety of looks that can be achieved, all using the same simple pattern units. You may have to look closely at some of the quilts to recognize the familiar shapes, but I assure you, they are all Storm at Sea variations!

Storm at Sea can be effectively combined with other pieced units, as Peggy Martin did in *Eye of the Storm*, page 40. Peggy is well known for her quick-strip paper-piecing method, which she used to construct the quilt's center. She then surrounded it with Storm at Sea units to create an undulating, medallion-style frame.

The project quilt *Under the (Storm at) Sea*, page 67, uses four-patches in the center of some Big SIS units to make the eyes of the fish.

The project quilt *Piñata*, page 63, uses Little SIS units as the center squares in the orange Big SIS blocks. Notice how this subdivision adds more movement to the project by breaking up the large center patch of the Big SIS blocks.

Standard Big SIS units

Big SIS units with center variation

TRIANGLE-IN-A-SQUARE (TIS) UNITS

Adding a line in the center of the rectangular Diamond unit effectively divides it into two equal squares. I call these TIS units, which is short for Triangle-in-a-Square. Look through any collection of traditional quilt blocks, and you will see this unit used over and over. Although it is technically not part of the traditional Storm at Sea pattern, two TIS units together make one Diamond unit, so it is very easy to make this substitution using either of the design grids. Plus, this versatile unit can be cut and pieced using the TRIMplate tool just as for the Diamonds (see Piecing with TRIMplates, page 25).

TIS unit

Two TIS units make one Diamond.

FROM DESIGN TO FABRIC

You have created a wonderful, unique design using one of the Storm at Sea grids, and you are ready to get to your fabric stash and begin. How much fabric you need depends on the size of the blocks and your chosen piecing method. All the projects in this book are based on these finished block sizes:

Diamond: 3" × 6"

Big SIS: 6" × 6"

Little SIS: 3" × 3"

piecing options

How you decide to piece your design depends on your personal preferences, skill level, and what tools you have available. I hope you are inspired to try my new TRIMplate piecing method as described on pages 25–35. TRIMplates are specially designed for cutting the patches and trimming up the finished units to the perfect size. This method is fast and produces accurate blocks using basic rotary cutting skills, and it is simple enough for beginners.

Foundation (paper) piecing is another option for making precise units. Full size patterns are provided on pages 76–77 for foundation piecing. You could also use these patterns to create templates for hand or machine piecing if you are skilled in these methods. A word of caution for beginners, however: traditional template piecing requires exact cutting, careful positioning, and precise sewing to produce consistently accurate finished blocks. This is especially important for the Diamond and Big SIS units. Little SIS units are easily pieced using the typical sew-and-flip method described on page 23.

See Resources, page 78, for ordering information for the following piecing-related products.

Quilters' TRIMplates

Carol Doak Teaches You to Paper Piece DVD

Piecing Tips & Tricks Tool

All-in-One Quilter's Reference Tool

Mastering Precision Piecing by Sally Collins

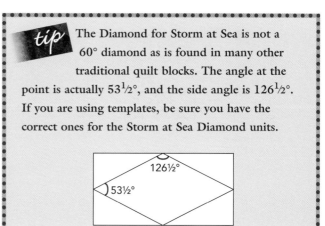

tip The Diamond for Storm at Sea is not a 60° diamond as is found in many other traditional quilt blocks. The angle at the point is actually 53½°, and the side angle is 126½°. If you are using templates, be sure you have the correct ones for the Storm at Sea Diamond units.

Planning Worksheet

	A ▢	B ◿	C ◺	D ◹	Dr ◹	E ◇	F ▢	G ▢	H ▢
☐ Fabric 1									
☐ Fabric 2									
☐ Fabric 3									
☐ Fabric 4									
☐ Fabric 5									
☐ Fabric 6									
☐ Fabric 7									
☐ Fabric 8									

estimating yardage for original designs

The easiest way to approach any of the patterns is to use multiple fabrics for each color on your design: the "scrappy" approach. This provides the most flexibility, and, best of all, you never run out of fabric!

A simple worksheet like the one above is helpful for more detailed planning.

Diamond Unit

Big SIS Unit

Little SIS Unit

TIS

To use the worksheet, paste a small swatch of fabric on each row or use colored pencils to indicate fabric color. Then count how many A, B, C, and so forth, pieces are in the design for each fabric and enter those numbers into the worksheet.

 tip For a complex design, counting all the patches can be tricky. Try doing just one row at a time, or make a copy of your original design and cross off each unit as you count.

To estimate yardage requirements, you need to know how many of each patch can be cut from a specific amount of fabric, such as one strip or one quarter yard. For TRIMplate piecing, these numbers are given in the charts on page 22. If you are using a different piecing method, you can make these calculations and build your own chart, or use a book such as the *All-in-One Quilter's Reference Tool*, available from C&T Publishing, to look up the appropriate numbers (see Resources, page 78).

TRIMplate piecing: using the charts

The following charts can be used to estimate yardage for the TRIMplate piecing method. Chart 1 shows what size square or rectangle to cut for each piece, and any necessary subcutting. For example, C triangles are cut from 4¼″ squares. The squares are cut in half once on the diagonal to yield two triangles per square.

Chart 2 indicates how many pieces can be cut from a quarter yard or a full-width (40″) strip of fabric. Quarter yards can be either a fat quarter (about 18″ × 20″) or a long quarter (about 9″ × 40″). For example, a quarter yard yields 44 B triangles and a strip 3½″ wide yields 22 B triangles.

For example, this design is made from the following units:

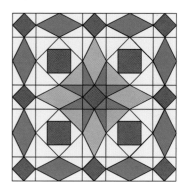

Make 1.

Make 8.

Make 4.

Make 4.

Make 8.

Cutting for TRIMplate Piecing—Chart 1

PIECE	CUT SIZE	UNIT
A, F ☐	3½″ ☐	Big SIS; Little SIS
B ◺	3½″ ◹	Big SIS
C ◺	4¼″ ◹	Big SIS
D & Dr ◺ ◿	2½″ × 5″ ▱	Diamond; TIS
E ◇	4″ × 7″ ☐	Diamond
G ☐	2″ ☐	Little SIS
H ☐	4″ ☐	TIS

Cutting for TRIMplate Piecing—Chart 2

PIECE	STRIP WIDTH	PATCHES PER STRIP	PATCHES PER QUARTER YARD
A, F	3½″	11 ☐	22 ☐
B	3½″	22 ◺	44 ◺
C	4¼″	18 ◺	32 ◺
D or Dr	2½″	16 ◺	48 ◺
D or Dr	5″ (option)	32 ◺	32 ◺
E	4″	5 ◇	8 ◇
E	7″ (option)	10 ◇	10 ◇
G	2″	20 ☐	80 ☐
H	4″	10 ☐	20 ☐

The number of individual pieces required have been entered into the worksheet.

Unit	Big SIS			Diamond			Little SIS	
	A	B ◿	C ◺	D ◺	Dr ◹	E ◇	F ☐	G ☐
Fabric 1	4						9	
Fabric 2				4	4	8		4
Fabric 3			4			4		
Fabric 4		16	12	20	20			32

Using Chart 2, ¼ yard or 2 strips 3½" wide are needed to cut the Fabric 1 A and F pieces, a total of 13 squares, 3½".

From Fabric 2: ¼ yard for the E pieces, plus 1 strip 2½" wide for the D and Dr pieces. The 4 G pieces can be cut from an additional 2" strip, or from the remainder of the 2½" strip.

From Fabric 3: 1 strip 4" wide for the E pieces, plus 1 strip 4¼" wide for the C pieces.

From Fabric 4: 1 strip 3½" wide for the B pieces, 1 strip 4¼" wide for the C pieces, ¼ yard for the D and Dr pieces, plus 2 strips 2" wide for the G pieces.

> **tip** Stay Organized! Use paper plates to organize the cut pieces. Label the plates A, B, C, and so forth, and put the appropriate pieces in them as they are cut to size. The plates are easy to stack and can then be slipped into a plastic bag to keep all the cut pieces together.

piecing little SIS units

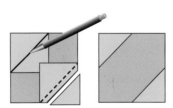

Little SIS unit

Finished size: 3″ × 3″

Piece F: cut 1 square 3½″ × 3½″

Piece G: cut 4 squares 2″ × 2″

1. Mark diagonal lines from corner to corner on the back of each G square. Position 2 G squares on opposite corners of F, right sides together; sew on the marked lines. Trim at least ¼" away from the seam to remove excess fabric from the corners; press toward the G's.

2. Repeat on the remaining corners with two more G squares. The unit should measure 3½" square.

To make partial Little SIS units, simply omit 1, 2, or 3 of the corner squares. The unpieced corners are then the same fabric as the center F square.

Partial Little SIS units

construction basics

JOINING THE UNITS

Once the units are pieced, joining them together is a matter of employing standard quilt construction techniques. The most important thing to consider is matching points in adjacent units. If you have pieced them accurately, this will not pose a problem for a quilter with some piecing experience. See Troubleshooting Storm at Sea Piecing, pages 34–35, for potential piecing problems and solutions.

1. Arrange the units and double-check that they have been pieced correctly and are oriented the right way to complete the pattern. I suggest using a vertical design wall for this, which can be as simple as a flannel-backed tablecloth attached to a closet door or wall.

2. To join 2 units together (such as a Diamond and a Big SIS), begin by pinning the points where the seams intersect. I use extra-fine pins or silk pins for this. Put the first pin in so it goes from the back of the first unit into the front of the second unit. Check that the pin comes out exactly at the point of the first unit. Leave this pin sticking straight up as you pin on either side and very close to the first pin to hold the units together. Remove the first pin.

Pin points where seams intersect.

PRESSING CONSIDERATIONS FOR STORM AT SEA UNITS

❖ Pressing pieced units properly is important for accurate finished units.

❖ Use a firm pressing surface with a cotton fabric cover.

❖ Use a dry iron to press after each seam. First, set the stitches by pressing the seam flat from the wrong side. Then, without moving the unit, open out the top piece and use the side of the iron to gently press into the seam. Check to be sure the seam is pressed well and that there is not a little pleat along the stitching line.

❖ When joining Storm at Sea units, press *away* from the Diamond units whenever possible. This tends to leave less bulk in the seam allowance.

❖ Sew units into rows and press the seam allowances to *one side*.

❖ Sew the rows together and press these final seams *open* to reduce bulk.

PIECING
WITH TRIMPLATES

the diamond unit/ TIS unit TRIMplate

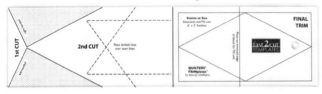

TRIMplate for Diamond Unit/TIS Unit

This TRIMplate is used to make Diamond units and Triangle-in-a-Square (TIS) units. This tool is different from other acrylic rulers and cutting guides you may have used before. Take a moment to familiarize yourself with it before you begin to cut. The TRIMplate has three separate areas on it. They are labeled "1st CUT," "2nd CUT," and "FINAL TRIM." Each area has a distinct function. Follow the directions step-by-step and pay particular attention to the position of the TRIMplate as you perform each step.

DIAMOND UNITS

Diamond unit

Cut size: 3½″ × 6½″

Finished size: 3″ × 6″

Each unit requires:

  2 D rectangles, 2½″ × 5″

  1 E rectangle, 4″ × 7″

1. Arrange pairs of D rectangles so that the *same sides* are together (right sides together or wrong sides together). Use a rotary cutter and ruler to cut the rectangles in half from corner to corner to yield 2 D triangles and 2 D-reverse (Dr) triangles.

Cut with same sides of fabric together.

> *tip* It doesn't matter which direction you cut the D's (bottom right to upper left or vice versa) as long as you always cut 2 at a time, with the same sides of the fabric together, either wrong sides or right sides together. Each pair of D rectangles yields a total of 4 D triangles, and 2 of them will be mirror images of the other 2. In other words, when you cut 1 pair of D rectangles, you are making enough D triangles to sew 1 complete Diamond unit.

2. Place the E rectangle on a cutting mat as shown, right side up. Turn the TRIMplate so the area labeled "1st CUT" is at the top. Rotate the TRIMplate so the right-handed shaded area covers the upper left corner of E. If you are left-handed, rotate the TRIMplate so the left-handed shaded area covers the upper right corner of E. Cut as shown to remove the fabric under the shaded area of the TRIMplate. *Discard* this small fabric triangle.

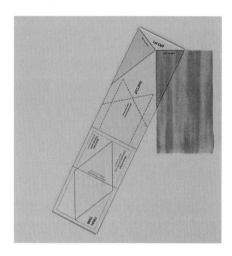

Right-handed position

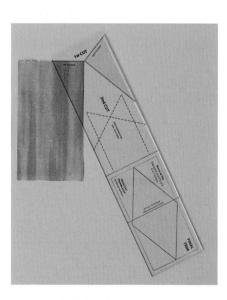

Left-handed position

3. Slide the TRIMplate out of the way and turn over piece E from side to side, as you would turn the page of a book, so the *back* (wrong) side of the fabric is face up. Reposition the TRIMplate as you did in the previous step and trim off the opposite corner. You have shaped one end of the diamond. **Stop! Do not shape the other end of the diamond yet!**

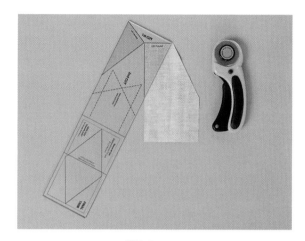

Trim off opposite corner.

One end of E is shaped.

4. Arrange the shaped E, 1 D, and 1 Dr as shown, all right sides up. Flip E to the left so it is on top of D and align the raw edges. Position the pieces so the tip of D extends *about ¼″* beyond the tip of E. This does not need to be exact. Sew with E on top.

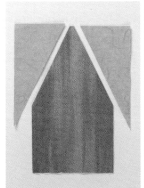  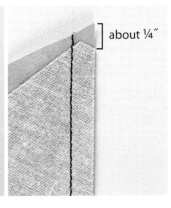

| Arrange pieces. | Sew with E on top. | Pieces are shown actual size. |

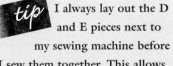

tip Here's something you won't find with most piecing methods: it is *not important* that the raw edges of D and E are lined up perfectly. What is important is that you sew with the edge of your ¼″ foot guiding along the cut edge of the E diamond. Remember, the E piece has been shaped to the proper angle that you want to preserve in the pieced unit. The D triangles are oversized and will be trimmed after sewing. There is no need to pin, and if the D triangle slips a bit as you sew, *it will not matter*, as long as you continue to guide your ¼″ seam from the edge of the E diamond.

tip I always lay out the D and E pieces next to my sewing machine before I sew them together. This allows me to double-check that I have the right fabric and that the pieces are turned the correct way.

5. Press the seam toward D, and then position Dr on top of the pieced unit so the tips of the 2 D's are about even.

6. Sew with Dr on top; press toward Dr.

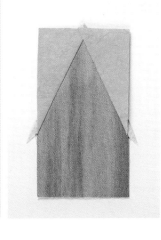

7. The opposite end of the Diamond is shaped in a different manner, this time using the "2nd CUT" area near the center of the TRIMplate. Position the pieced unit horizontally on the cutting mat so the point of E is on the left for right-handed cutting, and on the right for lefties. Rotate the TRIMplate as shown so a set of dashed lines is directly on top of the seams. Cut against the side of the TRIMplate to remove 1 corner of E.

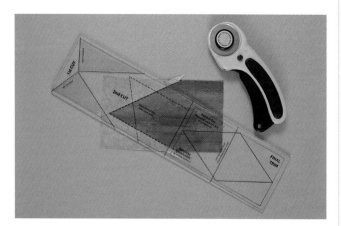

Second cut, right-handed position

8. Without moving the fabric, swivel the TRIMplate so the other set of dashed lines is directly on top of the seams. Cut off the remaining corner of E to finish shaping the diamond.

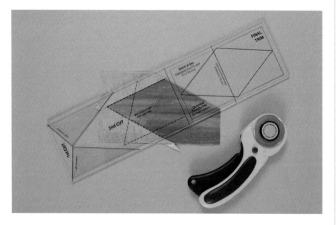

Swivel TRIMplate.

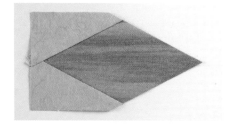

Shaped Diamond

tip The "2nd CUT" portion of the TRIMplate is one reason the finished Diamond units are so accurate. The dashed lines are positioned so the cut is the correct distance away from the previous seams. The $\frac{1}{4}$″ seam allowance is engineered into this distance, so in the following step it is important to sew with an accurate $\frac{1}{4}$″ seam allowance.

9. Arrange the remaining D and Dr next to the pieced unit. Position, sew, and press as in Steps 4 through 6 above.

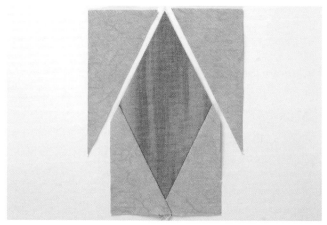

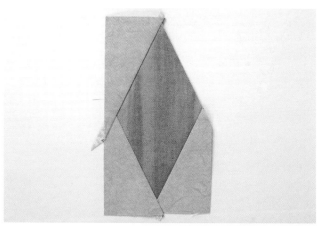

10. Position the "FINAL TRIM" section of the TRIMplate on top of the pieced unit so the angled lines are on top of the seams. Trim the excess fabric from 3 sides.

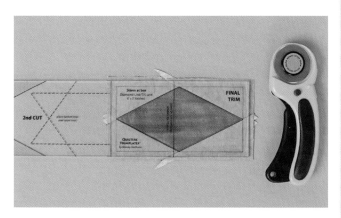

11. Rotate the pieced unit halfway around (180°) and reposition the TRIMplate to trim the fourth side to complete the unit. The unit should measure 3½″ × 6½″.

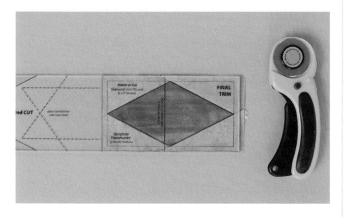

TRIANGLE-IN-A-SQUARE (TIS) UNITS

TIS unit

Cut size: 3½″ × 3½″

Finished size: 3″ × 3″

Each unit requires

    2 D rectangles, 2½″ × 5″
    (yields enough pieces for 2 units)

    1 H square, 4″ × 4″

1. Arrange and cut D rectangles into triangles as for the Diamond, Step 1, page 25.

2. Place the H square on a cutting mat, right side up. Turn the TRIMplate so the area labeled "1st CUT" is at the top. Rotate the TRIMplate so the shaded area covers the upper left corner of H. If you are left-handed, rotate the TRIMplate in the opposite direction, so the shaded area covers the upper right corner of H. Cut as shown to remove the fabric under the shaded area of the TRIMplate.

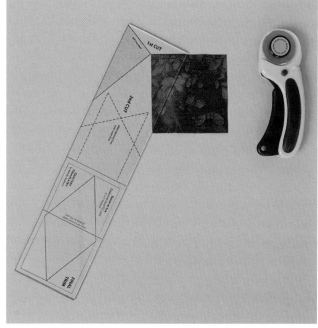

3. Slide the TRIMplate out of the way and turn over piece H from side to side, as you would turn the page of a book, so the *back* (wrong) side of the fabric is face up. Reposition the TRIMplate as you did in the previous step and trim off the opposite corner. The H triangle is now shaped. Be careful to keep the shaped end of the triangle facing away from you.

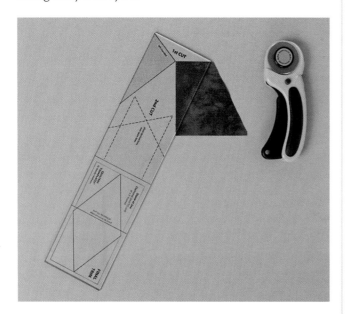

> *tip* It would be easy to accidentally turn H sideways. You may want to put a pin in the H triangle after it is shaped as a reminder. Position the pin so the tip of the pin points toward the top point of the triangle.

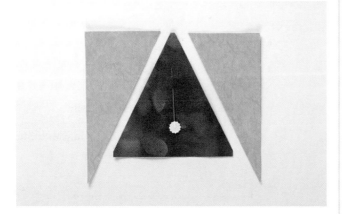

4. Arrange the shaped H, 1 D, and 1 Dr as shown above, right sides up. Flip H to the left so it is on top of D and align the raw edges.

5. Position the pieces so the tip of D extends about ¼˝ beyond the tip of H. *This does not need to be exact.* Sew with H on top.

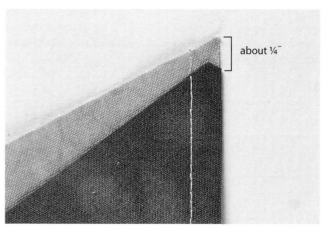

about ¼˝

6. Press the seam toward D, and then position Dr on top of the pieced unit so the tips of the 2 D's are about even. Sew with Dr on top; press toward Dr.

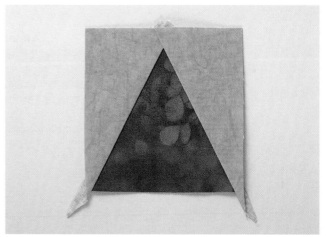

7. Position the "FINAL TRIM" section of the TRIMplate on top of the pieced unit so the angled lines are on top of the seams. Trim excess fabric from 3 sides.

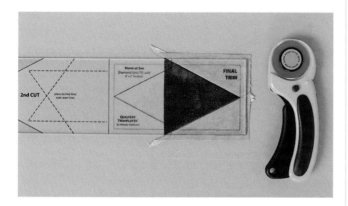

8. Rotate the pieced unit halfway around (180˚) and align the top edge of the unit on the line marked "Place on trimmed edge of block for TIS unit." (Don't pay any attention to the diagonal lines on the TRIMplate at this point.) Trim off the bottom edge so the TIS unit measures 3½" × 3½".

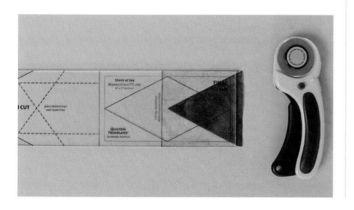

tip The seamlines on the trimmed unit are not supposed to end up directly in the corners. On a properly trimmed TIS unit, the seams will end on the bottom edge, about ⅛" in from the corner.

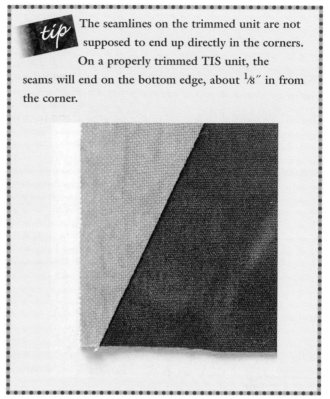

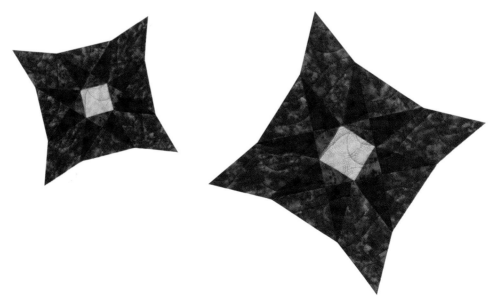

the big SIS unit TRIMplate

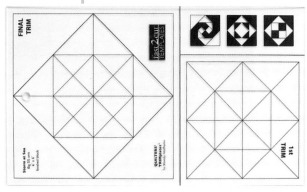

TRIMplate for Big SIS Unit

BIG SIS UNITS

Big SIS unit

Cut size: 6½″ × 6½″

Finished size: 6″ × 6″

Each unit requires

    1 A square, 3½″ × 3½″

    2 B squares, 3½″ × 3½″

    2 C squares, 4¼″ × 4¼″

1. Cut the B and C squares in half on the diagonal to make half-square triangles.

> *tip* The B and C squares do not need to be cut precisely. Remember, they are oversized and will be trimmed after sewing. It is faster if you stack several squares and cut them at the same time.

2. Roughly center the long side of a B triangle on the side of an A square. Sew with A on top. Repeat on the opposite side. Use an accurate ¼″ seam.

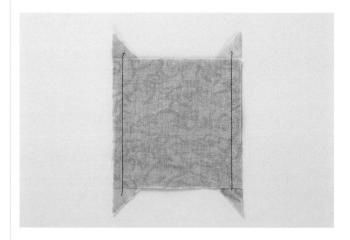

Big SIS unit with 2 sides sewn

> *tip* The exact position of the B triangle is not important, so you can center the pieces by eye. This is easier to see with the B triangle face up and the A square on top.

> *tip* It is *not important* that the raw edges of A and B are lined up perfectly. What is important is that you sew with the edge of your ¼″ foot guiding off the cut edge of the A square. There is no need to pin, and if the B triangle slips a bit as you sew, *it will not matter,* as long as you continue to guide your ¼″ seam from the edge of the A square.

3. Press away from the A square. Sew the remaining B triangles to A in the same manner; press away from A.

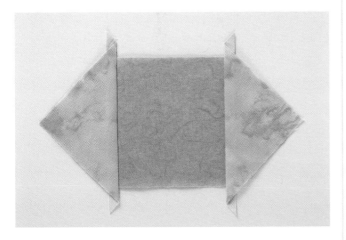

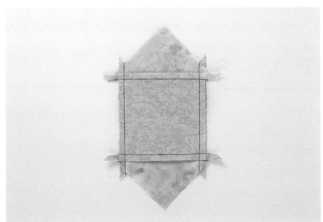

4. Position the section of the large TRIMplate labeled "1st TRIM" on top of the pieced unit so the diagonal lines are directly on top of the seamlines. Trim 2 sides; rotate the unit halfway and trim the remaining 2 sides.

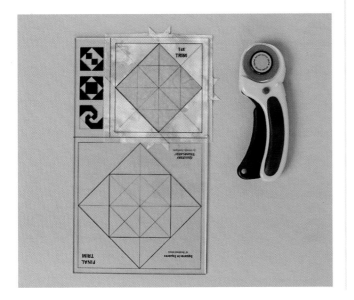

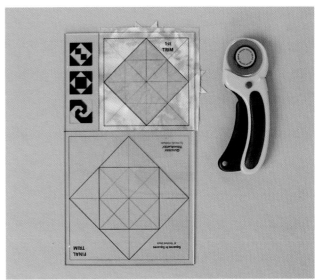

5. Add C triangles on all 4 sides as for the B triangles. Trim the completed unit using the "FINAL TRIM" section of the TRIMplate. Position the TRIMplate on top of the pieced unit, with the diagonal lines directly on top of the seamlines. Trim 2 sides; rotate the unit and trim the remaining 2 sides so the unit measures 6½" × 6½".

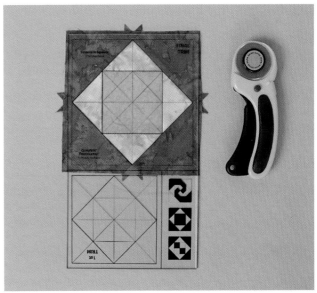

troubleshooting storm at sea piecing

Problem: The seams on the Diamond unit do not line up with the TRIMplate on the final trim step.

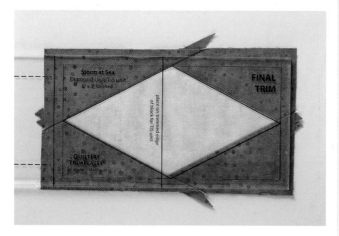

Problem with final trim

First of all, don't be overly critical! The TRIMplate shows even tiny variations in the finished unit. If a seamline or point is less than ⅛″ off, don't worry about it. Ask yourself if you will be able to pin and sew the offending point to the adjacent unit without distorting the quilt. In most cases you can reposition the TRIMplate for the final trim so that all 4 points of the Diamond fall as close as possible to where they are supposed to. In this way, you can "split the difference" on any variation in the unit, so no single point is too far off.

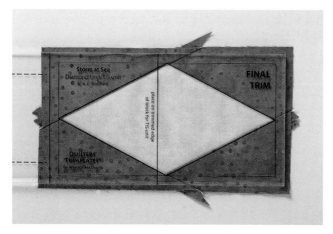

Reposition TRIMplate for final trim.

Solutions:

1. Did you remember to use the "2nd CUT" area of the TRIMplate to shape the second end of the Diamond? If you inadvertently shaped both ends of the diamond using the TRIMplate's "1st CUT" area, the seams will be in the wrong place when you do the final trim.

2. Check that the seams were pressed well, so there is no extra fabric folded over the seams. Press the seams all the way out, so the thread in the seamline is just barely visible from the front of the unit.

3. You may need to adjust your ¼″ seam slightly. If the seams fall *inside* the diagonal lines on the TRIMplate, make your seam allowance a little narrower: a scant ¼″. If the seams fall *outside* the TRIMplate lines, make your seam allowance a bit wider. You need to correct the seam allowance only for the *last* 2 triangles added, not the 2 triangles on the first end of the diamond.

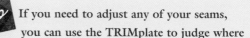
tip If you need to adjust any of your seams, you can use the TRIMplate to judge where the new seam needs to go. A seam correction should be *half* the distance you see from the front of the unit. For example, with the TRIMplate on top of the unit, the last seam is ⅛″ outside the line. Sew the new seam ¹⁄₁₆″ inside the first line of stitching. You can correct seams that are not quite at the right angle in the same way. Just remember to sew half the distance of the required correction.

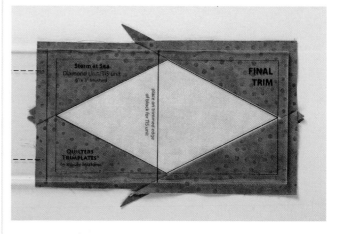

Last seam is ⅛″ outside TRIMplate line.

Re-sew seam ¹⁄₁₆″ inside first line of stitching.

Problem: Points are lost or there is a gap where 2 units are sewn together.

Missing points

Gap between points

The most important intersection is where the sides of 2 Diamond units touch or where a Diamond is sewn to a Big SIS. A misplaced seam could be very obvious here, especially with high-contrast fabrics. Take your time to pin and sew these intersections accurately for the best-looking finished piece. (See Joining the Units, page 24.)

Solutions:

1. Adjust the seam allowance so the line of stitching falls just barely **outside** the point where the seams cross.

2. At critical intersections, switch to a longer stitch length about ½″ before and after the point where the seams cross. Open and check the match; correct the seam if necessary. Switch back to standard stitch length and sew over the basting-length stitches.

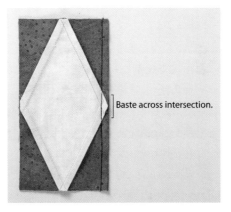

Baste across intersection.

3. If you are using a universal-style sewing machine needle, switch to a Microtex/sharp or jeans/denim needle. These have sharper points, which improve accuracy when sewing through multiple seam allowances.

Any Port in a Storm

72″ × 90″, Wendy Mathson, quilted by Faith Horsky.

Pieced with scraps as I experimented with the design of the Storm at Sea TRIMplates, this quilt was meant to be a throwaway. As it got larger I began to like it more and more, and now it is one of my favorites, particularly the border variation. The paper-pieced lighthouse block is a pattern from *Shoreline Quilts*, by Cyndy Lyle Rymer, C&T Publishing.

Dawn Is Breaking

49″ × 52″, Jan LaGrone.

Jan's very first quilt was a feathered star, made in 2004 in one of my adult education classes. It didn't take long for her to progress to designing and machine quilting her own original quilts.

Calm Before the Storm

58″ × 58″, Barbara Friedman.

This began as a workshop project, but Barbara's color choices and fabric placement made it totally different from the class sample.

Beacons in the Storm

60″ × 60″, Lorraine Marstall, quilted by Lorrie Ayala.

A double diamond setting gave Lorraine the perfect way to use her Lee Ann batik lighthouse fabric. Three of the corner lighthouses are paper-pieced adaptations from patterns in *Shoreline Quilts*, by Cyndy Lyle Rymer, C&T Publishing.

Stormy Weather

30″ × 30″, Allegra "Lee" Olsen.

Lee added appliqué, beads, and three-dimensional folded flowers on top of the colorful Storm at Sea units. Lee entered this piece as part of a fabric challenge by Eccentrix Dyeworks.

Eye of the Storm

66½″ × 66½″, Peggy Martin.

Peggy pieced the circular center section using her own quick-strip paper-piecing method, with Storm at Sea units surrounding it medallion-style with waves of color.

Three Hearts = A Stormy Relationship?

43″ × 33″, Lisa Coulombe and Wendy Mathson

This was a happy collaboration between friends. Lisa selected the fabrics to piece and masterfully quilt one of my designs.

Castle Garden

36″ × 36″, Sandy Harper, quilted by Faith Horsky.

Sandy was inspired to play with the double diamond design grid to come up with her unique variation.

Radiant Beams

38″ × 38″, by Wendy Mathson, quilted by Faith Horsky.

Compare this quilt to *Beyond the Storm*. Can you see that they use the same pieced units? Only the color placement is different.

Beyond the Storm

33″ × 33″, Wendy Mathson, quilted by Faith Horsky.

The outer border was changed to make a variation of the workshop sample.

Gemstones

62″ × 62″, Jeralyn Dunn, quilted by Joy Duessen.

Notice how Jeralyn changed the centers of some of her Big SIS blocks to four-patches. She also rearranged the units near the outer edge so they are different from the standard grid.

Storm at Sea—Category 5

40″ × 48″, Patricia Wolfe.

Pat made the center part of this piece in my workshop to learn the TRIMplate piecing method. She decided to cut it up and raw-edge appliqué it to the dark background. With the addition of silver metallic clouds and sashiko-style hand stitching to depict rain, Pat thought it was perfect for her friendship group's water-themed challenge.

It Was a Dark and Stormy Night

38½″ × 38½″, Wendy Mathson, quilted by Faith Horsky.

Turning the design on point gives it a whole new look. Black polished cotton on the outer border shows off the expert machine quilting by my friend Faith.

Storm at Tiffany's Winery

41″ × 41″, Collette McManus

Collette's starting point was a multi-color grapevine print that looks like Tiffany-style stained glass.

Summerfest Garden Party

88½″ × 67½″, designed by Joen Wolfrom, pieced by Jeanne Lounsbury, and machine quilted by Karen Dovala.

This was the cover quilt for Joen's book *A Garden Party of Quilts,* C&T Publishing.

Genesis, Exodus

27½″ × 27½″, Wendy Mathson.

This was the first nontraditional Storm at Sea quilt I designed, so it was a beginning and a departure for me. This became my workshop sample to be used as a teaching tool.

Diamond Symmetry

27″ × 27″, Linda Kamm.

Linda used basically the same colors in this wallhanging as in *Genesis, Exodus* (above), but fabric placement and a different border give this piece a much different look.

With Spoiled Dogs, You Make Headboards, Not Bed Quilts

69˝× 70˝, Linda Kamm.

Linda designed this to hang on the wall above her bed as a headboard. (And yes, her two dogs may be a bit spoiled, but they're absolutely adorable.)

Tropical Storm

52″ × 61″, Linda Kamm.

Not only is she a talented designer, Linda is also a professional machine quilter. This piece is exquisitely quilted with fanciful motifs in silver metallic thread.

Flight

30½″ × 30½″, Sandy Harper

Asymmetrical fabric placement and skillful use of color evoke images of soaring birds.

Storm Surge/Power Surge jacket, Wendy Mathson.

A Storm at Sea jacket seemed appropriate to wear for guild lectures. I used the standard grid to design the front and sleeves, and the double diamond grid for the back to give it a different set of curves.

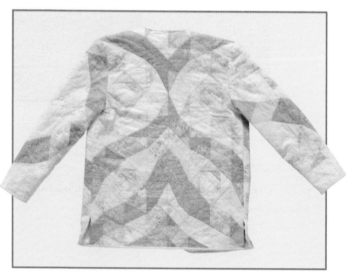

Back view of jacket

Flights of Fancy

48½″ × 56½″, Patricia Wolfe, quilted by Jan McMurray.

The squares were fussy cut to show off the colorful birds and insects in the fabric.
Careful color arrangement imparts a glowing center to Pat's quilt.

Serengeti Storm

62″ × 79″, Jan LaGrone and Linda Kamm.

Beginning with Linda's sketch and my fabric, Jan pieced and machine quilted this African-themed beauty. Along the way Jan, Linda, and I changed some fabrics and enlarged it to be a bed-sized quilt.

GIRAFFE IN MOTION

Designed by Wendy Mathson; pieced by Wendy Mathson and Faith Horsky;
quilted by Faith Horsky and Linda Kamm.

FINISHED QUILT: 72½˝ × 81½˝

This quilt was begun as a fairly predictable dark/light scrap quilt using the Little SIS variation to form stars. My friend Faith Horsky undertook the task of putting this together as a challenge to use as many "ugly greens" as possible from my scrap collection. She added some "uglies" of her own but decided the quilt was too boring to finish. We agreed that it needed some sort of focal point. Not long after Faith returned the unfinished top to me, I found the silk-screened giraffe panel at a quilt show. I removed a few pieced units and added the panel, which inspired me to design the spiky Diamond and Little SIS border. It's not boring anymore!

Big SIS Diamond Little SIS

Pieces Needed

Materials and Cutting for TRIMplate Piecing or Foundation Piecing

Cut all strips across width of fabric; subcut if indicated.
Numbers in parentheses represent additional pieces needed to make quilt
without the focus panel.

FABRIC	YARDAGE	CUT
Focus panel	15½″ square	15½″ square
Assorted greens	4¼ yards total	38 (42) A squares 3½″ 29 (30) F squares 3½″ 76 (84) C squares 4¼″ 97 (101) E rectangles 4″ × 7″
Orange	½ yard	3 strips 3½″; subcut into 26 (30) F squares 3½″
Off-white	4¼ yards	7 (8) strips 3½″; subcut into 76 (84) B squares 3½″ 11 strips 5″; subcut into 164 (172) rectangles 2½″ × 5″ for D pieces 11 strips 2″; subcut into 216 G squares 2″ 5 strips 6½″ for pieced border
Tan	1¾ yards	2 strips 5″; subcut into 30 rectangles 2½″ × 5″ for D pieces 6 strips 3½″ for pieced border 9 strips 2″ for outer border
Binding fabric	⅝ yard	2″-strip width double-fold binding
Backing fabric	5 yards	
Batting	76½″ × 85½″	

Pieces Needed

Unit	Big SIS			Diamond			Little SIS	
FINISHED SIZE	6″ × 6″			3″ × 6″			3″ × 3″	
Pieces Needed	A ▢	B ◺	C ◹	D ◣	Dr ◿	E ◇	F ▢	G ▢
Assorted greens	38 (42)		152 (168)			97 (101)	29 (30)	
Orange							26	
Off-white		152 (168)		164 (172)	164 (172)			216 (220)
Tan				30	30			

unit assembly

You can either use the foundation template patterns, page 76, to make the units or use the Quilters' TRIMplates and refer to the TRIMplates Piecing section (pages 25–35). The Quilters' TRIMplates are available from C&T Publishing (see Resources, page 78).

Make 30.   Make 67 (71).

Diamond units

Make 38 (42).

Big SIS units

Make 22.   Make 29 (30).

Little SIS units

Make 4.

Partial Little SIS units

border assembly

1. Sew a 3½″ tan strip to a 6½″ off-white strip to make a strip set. Make 5 strip sets like this. Cut the strip sets into 26 border units 6½″ wide.

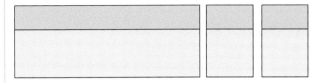

Make 5 strip sets. Cut into 6½″ segments.

2. Cut 4 off-white corner squares 3½″ × 3½″ from the leftover portion of a strip set.

3. Cut 4 rectangles 3½″ × 6½″ and 4 squares 3½″ × 3½″ from the remaining 3½″ tan strip.

4. Sew the tan and off-white squares together, and then sew the squares to the tan rectangles to make 4 border corners.

Make 4 border corners.

5. Refer to the quilt assembly diagram, page 56, to arrange and sew the appropriate Diamond units, Little SIS units, and border units into 2 side borders. See Construction Basics, page 24, for arrangement and pressing instructions.

6. Refer to the quilt assembly diagram to arrange and sew the appropriate Diamond units, Little SIS units, border units, and border corners into a top and bottom border.

quilt construction

1. Refer to the quilt assembly diagram and arrange the pieced Storm at Sea units into rows.

2. Sew the units into rows; press the seams away from the Diamond units. Sew the rows together; press the seams open.

3. Sew the side borders; press, then sew the top and bottom borders to the quilt; press.

4. For the outer border, measure the quilt horizontally. Sew 2"-wide tan strips together end-to-end, then cut 2 strips to the measured length. Sew the strips to the top and bottom of the quilt. Press toward the strips.

5. Measure the quilt top vertically, including the borders just added. Sew the remaining tan strips together end-to-end, then cut 2 strips to the measured length. Sew the strips to the sides of the quilt. Press.

6. Layer quilt top, batting and backing. Baste. Quilt as desired. Add binding.

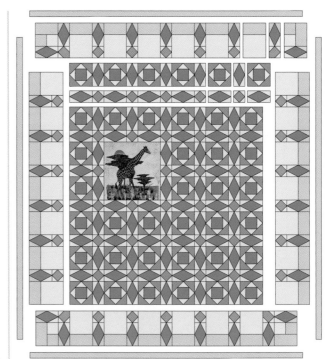

Quilt assembly diagram

RED SKY AT MORNING

Designed by Wendy Mathson; pieced by Michelle "Chellee" Mathson; quilted by Faith Horsky.

FINISHED QUILT: 39½" × 39½"

My 23-year-old daughter came home for a visit as I was finishing the projects for this book. Chellee had pieced several quilts before, but I had never shown her how to use my TRIMplates. After about 10 minutes of instruction, she was confident enough to make the units for this delightful wallhanging: her very first quilt using the TRIMplate piecing method!

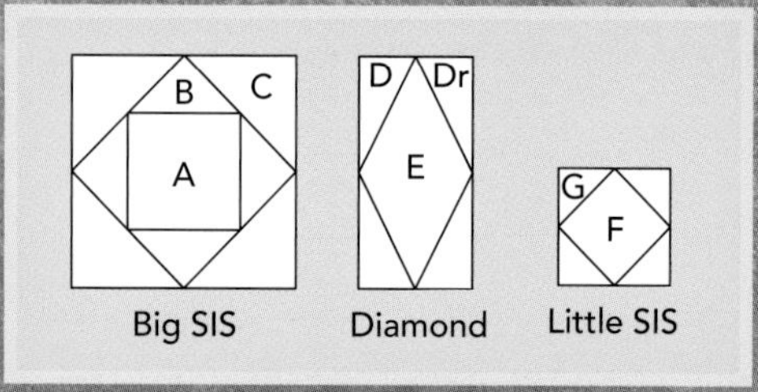

Big SIS   Diamond   Little SIS

Materials and Cutting for TRIMplate Piecing or Foundation Piecing
Cut all strips across width of fabric; subcut if indicated.

FABRIC	YARDAGE	CUT
Red	1⅜ yards	1 strip 3½″; subcut into 8 squares 3½″ for B pieces 2 strips 4¼″; subcut into 14 squares 4¼″ for C pieces 2 strips 5″; subcut into 28 rectangles 2½″ × 5″ for D pieces 1 strip 4″; subcut into 4 rectangles 4″ × 7″ for E pieces 2 strips 2″; subcut into 24 G squares 2″
Medium blue	1 yard	1 strip 3½″; subcut into 4 squares 3½″ for B pieces 1 strip 4¼″; subcut into 2 squares 4¼″ for C pieces 2 strips 5″; subcut into 20 rectangles 2½″ × 5″ for D pieces 1 strip 2″; subcut into 20 G squares 2″
Orange-pink	1⅛ yards	2 strips 4¼″; subcut into 10 squares 4¼″ for C pieces 1 strip 2½″; subcut into 4 rectangles 2½″ × 5″ for D pieces 3 strips 4″; subcut into 12 rectangles 4″ × 7″ for E pieces 1 strip 2″; subcut into 8 G squares 2″
Gold	¾ yard	1 strip 2½″; subcut into 4 rectangles 2½″ × 5″ for D pieces 1 strip 7″; subcut into 8 rectangles 4″ × 7″ for E pieces 1 strip 3½″; subcut into 9 F squares 3½″
Dark blue	2 yards	5 strips 3½″; subcut into 16 A squares 3½″, 20 squares 3½″ for B pieces, and 16 F squares 3½″ 1 strip 4¼″; subcut into 6 squares 4¼″ for C pieces 2 strips 5″; subcut into 24 rectangles 2½″ × 5″ for D pieces 2 strips 7″; subcut into 16 rectangles 4″ × 7″ for E pieces 1 strip 2″; subcut into 8 G squares 2″
Binding fabric	⅓ yard	2″-strip width double-fold binding
Backing fabric	2½ yards	
Batting	43½″ × 43½″	

Pieces Needed

Unit	Big SIS			Diamond			Little SIS	
FINISHED SIZE	6″ × 6″			3″ × 6″			3″ × 3″	
Pieces Needed	A	B	C	D	Dr	E	F	G
Red		16	28	28	28	4		24
Medium blue		8	4	20	20			20
Orange-pink			20	4	4	12		8
Gold				4	4	8	9	
Dark blue	16	40	12	24	24	16	16*	8

*Includes 4 squares 3½″ of color F for corners.

unit assembly

You can either use the foundation template patterns, page 76, to make the units or use the Quilters' TRIMplates and refer to the TRIMplates Piecing section. The Quilters' TRIMplates are available from C&T Publishing (see Resources, page 78).

Make 16.   Make 12.   Make 4.   Make 4.   Make 4.

Diamond units

Make 8.   Make 4.   Make 4.

Big SIS units

Make 4.   Make 4.   Make 1.

Little SIS units

Make 12.

Partial Little SIS unit

quilt construction

1. Refer to the quilt assembly diagram, page 59, and arrange the pieced Storm at Sea units into rows.

2. Sew the units into rows; press the seams away from the Diamond units. Sew the rows together; press the seams open.

3. Layer the quilt top, batting, and backing. Baste. Quilt as desired. Add sleeve and binding.

Quilt assembly diagram

Alternate color scheme:

Keep on the Sunny Side, Wendy Mathson, quilted by Lois Russell.

MANLY CURVES

Designed, pieced, and quilted by Wendy Mathson.

FINISHED QUILT: 61½˝ × 79½˝

 I made this quilt for my son, Scott, using "manly fabrics" in some of his favorite colors.

Big SIS

Diamond

Little SIS

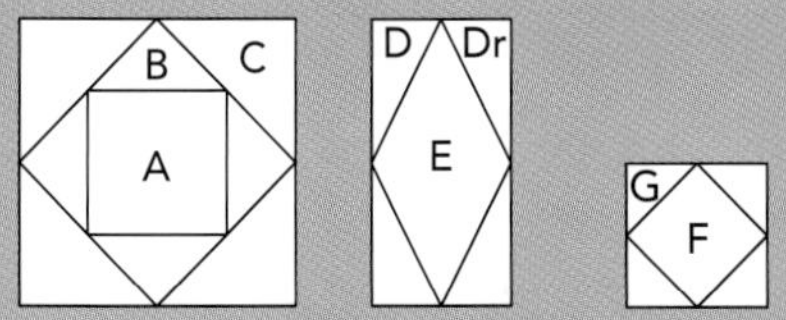

Materials and Cutting for TRIMplate Piecing or Foundation Piecing

Cut all strips across width of fabric; subcut if indicated.

FABRIC	YARDAGE	CUT
Light tan	1⅝ yards	7 strips 7˝; subcut into 70 rectangles 4˝ × 7˝ for E pieces
Gray	1½ yards	7 strips 4¼˝; subcut into 60 squares 4¼˝ for C pieces
		1 strip 7˝; subcut into 8 rectangles 4˝ × 7˝ for E pieces
		1 strip 2˝; subcut into 20 G squares 2˝
Blue batik	1 yard	2 strips 3½˝; subcut into 10 A squares 3½˝ and 10 F squares 3½˝
		1 strip 4¼˝; subcut into 8 squares 4¼˝ for C pieces
		7 strips 2˝ for inner border
Dark blue	1 yard	2 strips 3½˝; subcut into 20 squares 3½˝ for B pieces
		2 strips 5˝; subcut into 22 rectangles 2½˝ × 5˝ for D pieces
		1 strip 4˝; subcut into 4 rectangles 4˝ × 7˝ for E pieces
Dark brown	⅝ yard	5 strips 3½˝; subcut into 50 squares 3½˝ for B pieces
Brown print	1⅛ yards	3 strips 3½˝; subcut into 25 A squares 3½˝
		1 strip 4¼˝; subcut into 2 squares 4¼˝ for C pieces
		8 strips 2˝; subcut into 152 G squares 2˝
Taupe print	½ yard	4 strips 3½˝; subcut into 38 F squares 3½˝
Light brown	2⅝ yards	10 strips 5˝; subcut into 143 rectangles 2½˝ × 5˝ for D pieces
		7 strips 5½˝ for outer border
Binding fabric	½ yard	2˝ strip width double-fold binding
Backing fabric	4¾ yards	
Batting	65½˝ × 83½˝	

Pieces Needed

Unit	Big SIS			Diamond			Little SIS	
FINISHED SIZE	6˝ × 6˝			3˝ × 6˝			3˝ × 3˝	
Pieces Needed	A	B	C	D	Dr	E	F	G
Light tan						70		
Gray			120			8		20
Blue batik	10		16				10	
Dark blue		40		21	22	4		
Dark brown		100						
Brown print	25		4					152
Taupe print							38	
Light brown				143	142			

unit assembly

You can either use the foundation template patterns, page 76, to make the units or use the Quilters' TRIMplates and refer to the TRIMplates Piecing section (pages 25–35). The Quilters' TRIMplates are available from C&T Publishing (see Resources, page 78).

Make 4. Make 4. Make 4. Make 4.

Make 39. Make 13. Make 14.

Diamond units

Make 25. Make 6. Make 4.

Big SIS units

Make 38.

Little SIS units

Make 10.

Partial Little SIS units

quilt construction

1. Refer to the quilt assembly diagram and arrange the pieced Storm at Sea units into rows.

2. Sew the units into rows; press the seams away from the Diamond units. Sew the rows together; press the seams open.

3. For the inner border, measure the quilt horizontally. Sew 2"-wide blue batik strips together end-to-end, then cut 2 strips to the measured length. Sew the strips to the top and bottom of the quilt. Press toward the strips.

4. Measure the quilt top vertically, including the borders just added. Sew the remaining blue batik strips together end-to-end, then cut 2 strips to the measured length. Sew the strips to the sides of the quilt. Press.

5. Repeat Steps 3 and 4 with 5½"-wide light brown strips to add the outer borders in the same manner.

6. Layer quilt top, batting, and backing. Baste. Quilt as desired. Add binding.

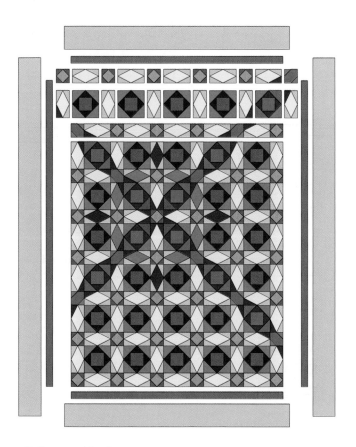

Quilt assembly diagram

Designed and pieced by Wendy Mathson; quilted by Faith Horsky.

FINISHED QUILT: 42½″ × 42½″

This variation features a slightly different arrangement of the standard Storm at Sea units, plus four TIS (Triangle-in-a-Square) units added in the center.

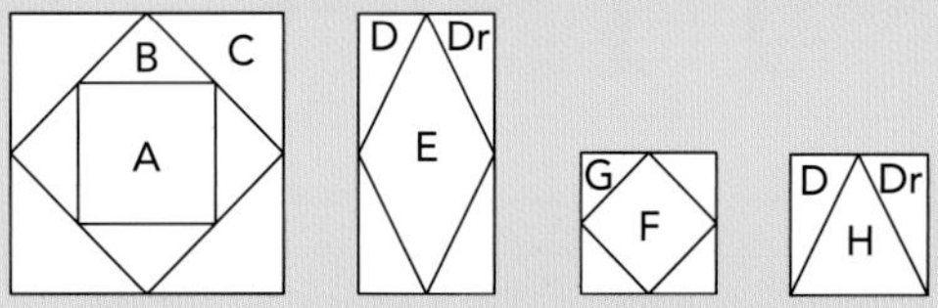

Big SIS   Diamond   Little SIS   TIS

Materials and Cutting for TRIMplate Piecing or Foundation Piecing
Cut all strips across width of fabric; subcut if indicated.

FABRIC NEEDED	YARDAGE	CUT
Assorted lime greens	2¼ yards total	12 A squares 3½″ 24 squares 3½″ for B pieces 14 squares 4¼″ for C pieces 52 rectangles 2½″ × 5″ for D pieces 16 rectangles 4″ × 7″ for E pieces 48 G squares 2″
Dark green	1 yard	2 strips 4¼″; subcut into 14 squares 4¼″ for C pieces 1 strip 5″; subcut into 12 rectangles 2½″ × 5″ for D pieces 5 strips 2″ for outer borders
Bright multicolor print	½ yard	1 strip 7″; subcut into 8 rectangles 4″ × 7″ for E pieces
Red	½ yard	1 strip 2½″; subcut into 8 rectangles 2½″ × 5″ for D pieces 1 strip 2″; subcut into 4 G squares 2″ 1 strip 4″; subcut into 4 H squares 4″
Red-orange	⅝ yard	2 strips 3½″; subcut into 8 squares 3½″ for B pieces and 5 F squares 3½″ 1 strip 2½″; subcut into 8 rectangles 2½″ × 5″ for D pieces 1 strip 2″; subcut into 8 G squares 2″
Orange	¾ yard	1 strip 4¼″; subcut into 4 squares 4¼″ for C pieces 2 strips 3½″; subcut into 12 F squares 3½″ 1 strip 2″; subcut into 8 G squares 2″
Yellow-orange	⅜ yard	1 strip 3½″; subcut into 4 F squares 3½″ 2 strips 2″; subcut into 24 G squares 2″
Red-violet	⅝ yard	1 strip 7″; subcut into 8 rectangles 4″ × 7″ for E pieces 1 strip 3½″; subcut into 4 F squares 3½″
Violet	¾ yard	1 strip 2½″; subcut into 4 rectangles 2½″ × 5″ for D pieces 1 strip 7″; subcut into 8 rectangles 4″ × 7″ for E pieces 1 strip 2″; subcut into 8 G squares 2″
Binding fabric	⅓ yard	2″-strip width double-fold binding
Backing fabric	2⅝ yards	
Batting	46½″ × 46½″	

Pieces Needed

Pieces Needed	Big SIS 6″ × 6″			Diamond 3″ × 6″			Little SIS 3″ × 3″		TIS 3″ × 3″
	A	B	C	D	Dr	E	F	G	H
Assorted lime greens	12	48	28	52*	52*	16		48	
Dark green			28	12	12				
Bright multicolor print						8			
Red				8	8			4	4
Red-orange		16		8	8		5	8	
Orange			8				12	8	
Yellow-orange							4	24	
Red-violet						8	4		
Violet				4	4	8		8	

*Includes 4 pieces each D and Dr for the TIS unit

unit assembly

You can either use the foundation template patterns, page 76, to make the units or use the Quilters' TRIMplates and refer to the specific TRIMplates Piecing section referenced with each step. The Quilters' TRIMplates are available from C&T Publishing (see Resources, page 78).

Make 4.   Make 4.   Make 4.   Make 4.   Make 4.

Make 4.   Make 4.   Make 4.   Make 4.

Diamond units

Make 4.
TIS units

Make 4.   Make 4.   Make 4.   Make 4.   Make 4.   Make 1.

Little SIS units

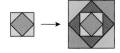

Make 4;   Make 4.
use as centers for
the 4 Big SIS units.

Big SIS units

quilt construction

1. Refer to the quilt assembly diagram and arrange the pieced Storm at Sea units into rows.

2. Sew the units into rows; press the seams to one side. Sew the rows together; press the seams open.

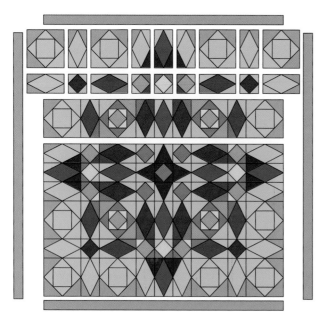

Quilt assembly diagram

3. For the border, measure the quilt horizontally. Sew 2"-wide dark lime green strips together end-to-end, then cut 2 strips to the measured length. Sew the strips to the top and bottom of the quilt. Press toward the strips.

4. Measure the quilt top vertically, including the borders just added. Sew the remaining dark lime green strips together end-to-end, then cut 2 strips to the measured length. Sew the strips to the sides of the quilt. Press.

5. Layer quilt top, batting, and backing. Baste. Quilt as desired. Add sleeve and binding.

Alternate color scheme:

Piñata Variation,
Jeralyn Dunn, quilted by
Joy Deussen. Jeralyn's
choice of low-contrast
fabrics in this lovely
variation reminds me
more of a lily pond than
a piñata.

UNDER THE
(STORM AT) SEA

Designed and quilted by Linda Kamm; pieced by Wendy Mathson.

FINISHED QUILT: 54$\frac{1}{2}$″ × 54$\frac{1}{2}$″

 I just couldn't resist the fanciful fish in Linda's original design. Her masterful machine quilting features bubbles, fish scales, and seaweed tendrils that emphasize the watery atmosphere of this undersea world.

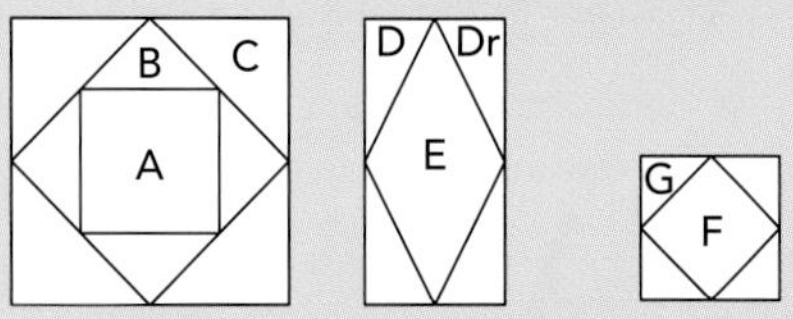

Big SIS   Diamond   Little SIS

Materials and Cutting for TRIMplate Piecing or Foundation Piecing
Cut all strips across width of fabric; subcut if indicated.

FABRIC	YARDAGE	CUT
Light orange	1⅞ yards	2 strips 3½˝; subcut into 12 A squares 3½˝ and 6 squares 3½˝ for B pieces 2 strips 4¼˝; subcut into 12 squares 4¼˝ for C pieces 2 strips 5˝; subcut into 28 rectangles 2½˝ × 5˝ for D pieces 2 strips 7˝; subcut into 20 E rectangles 4˝ × 7˝ for E pieces 3 strips 2˝; subcut into 44 G squares 2˝
Dark orange	¼ yard	1 strip 3½˝; subcut into 5 A squares 3½˝ and 2 squares 3½˝ for B pieces
Dark teal	1¾ yards	4 strips 3½˝; subcut into 4 A squares 3½˝, 8 squares 3½˝ for B pieces, and 32 F squares 3½˝ 1 strip 4¼˝; subcut into 2 squares 4¼˝ for C pieces 2 strips 5˝; subcut into 28 rectangles 2½˝ × 5˝ for D pieces 1 strip 4˝; subcut into 4 rectangles 4˝ × 7˝ for E pieces 3 strips 2˝; subcut into 48 G squares 2˝
Medium teal	1¾ yards	1 strip 4¼˝; subcut into 4 squares 4¼˝ for C pieces 2 strips 5˝; subcut into 32 rectangles 2½˝ × 5˝ for D pieces 2 strips 7˝; subcut into 16 rectangles 4˝ × 7˝ for E pieces 2 strips 3½˝; subcut into 16 F squares 3½˝ 2 strips 2˝; subcut into 36 G squares 2˝
Light teal	2 yards	3 strips 3½˝; subcut into 32 squares 3½˝ for B pieces 3 strips 4¼˝; subcut into 26 squares 4¼˝ for C pieces 2 strips 5˝; subcut into 20 rectangles 2½˝ × 5˝ for D pieces 1 strip 4˝; subcut into 4 rectangles 4˝ × 7˝ for E pieces 2 strips 6½˝; subcut into 8 squares 6½˝ for border
Light blue	1⅞ yards	2 strips 3½˝; subcut into 2 squares 3½˝ for B pieces and 16 F squares 3½˝ 1 strip 4¼˝; subcut into 6 squares 4¼˝ for C pieces 3 strips 5˝; subcut into 36 rectangles 2½˝ × 5˝ for D pieces 2 strips 7˝; subcut into 20 rectangles 4˝ × 7˝ for E pieces 1 strip 2˝; subcut into 20 G squares 2˝
Binding fabric	½ yard	2˝-strip width double-fold binding
Backing fabric	3½ yards	
Batting	58½˝ × 58½˝	

Unit	Big SIS			Diamond			Little SIS	
FINISHED SIZE	6˝ × 6˝			3˝ × 6˝			3˝ × 3˝	
Pieces Needed	A	B	C	D	Dr	E	F	G
Light orange	12	12	24	28	28	20		44*
Dark orange	5	4						
Dark teal	4	16	4	12	28	4	32	48
Medium teal			8	32	32	16	16	36*
Light teal		64	52	20	8	4		
Light blue		4	12	36	32	20	16	20

*Includes squares for the center of 4 Big SIS units

unit assembly

You can either use the foundation template patterns, page 76, to make the units or use the Quilters' TRIMplates and refer to the TRIMplates Piecing section (pages 25–25). The Quilters' TRIMplates are available from C&T Publishing (see Resources, page 78).

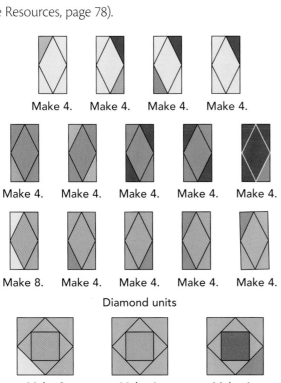
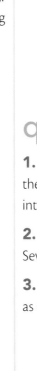
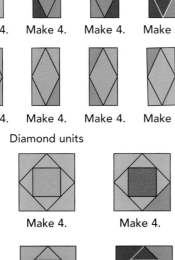

Diamond units

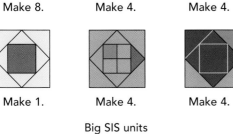

Big SIS units

Make 4.
Little SIS units

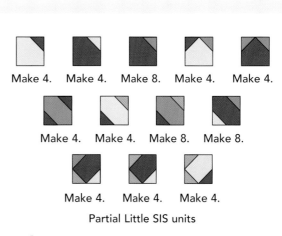

Partial Little SIS units

quilt construction

1. Refer to the quilt assembly diagram and arrange the pieced Storm at Sea units and 6½˝ light teal squares into rows.

2. Sew the units into rows; press the seams to one side. Sew the rows together; press the seams open.

3. Layer the quilt top, batting, and backing. Baste. Quilt as desired. Add sleeve and binding.

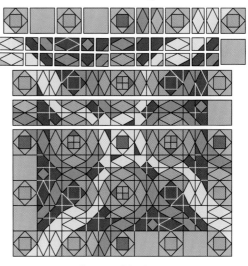

Quilt assembly diagram

PURELY ORNAMENTAL

Designed and pieced by Wendy Mathson; quilted by Sherrie Gwynn Smith.

FINISHED QUILT: 48½″ × 48½″

 Three-dimensional gold bows and tassels make these ornaments look even more festive. Sherrie's elegant quilting in gold metallic thread adds additional sheen to the borders and the pieced ribbons.

Materials and Cutting for TRIMplate Piecing or Foundation Piecing
Cut all strips across width of fabric; subcut if indicated.

FABRIC	YARDAGE	CUT
Assorted light golds	2½ yards total	8 squares 3½″ for B pieces 2 squares 4¼″ for C pieces 64 rectangles 2½″ × 5″ for D pieces 20 rectangles 4″ × 7″ for E pieces 24 F squares 3½″ 46 G squares 2″ 10 squares 6½″ 4 rectangles 3½″ × 6½″
Assorted dark metallic golds	1½ yards total	6 A squares 3½″ 8 F squares 3½″ 4 squares 3½″ for B pieces 2 squares 4¼″ for C pieces 14 rectangles 2½″ × 5″ for D pieces 6 rectangles 4″ × 7″ for E pieces 30 G squares 2″
Dark red batik	¾ yard	1 strip 2½″; subcut into 4 rectangles 2½″ × 5″ for D pieces 1 strip 4″; subcut into 4 rectangles 4″ × 7″ for E pieces 1 strip 3½″; subcut into 4 F squares 3½″ 1 strip 2″; subcut into 20 G squares 2″
Dark green batik	¾ yard	1 strip 2½″; subcut into 4 rectangles 2½″ × 5″ for D pieces 1 strip 4″; subcut into 4 rectangles 4″ × 7″ for E pieces 1 strip 3½″; subcut into 4 F squares 3½″ 1 strip 2″; subcut into 20 G squares 2″
Medium red metallic	¾ yard	1 strip 3½″; subcut into 2 squares 3½″ for A pieces 1 strip 4¼″; subcut into 4 squares 4¼″ for C pieces 1 strip 4″; subcut into 4 rectangles 4″ × 7″ for E pieces
Medium green metallic	¾ yard	1 strip 3½″; subcut into 2 squares 3½″ for A pieces 1 strip 4¼″; subcut into 4 squares 4¼″ for C pieces 1 strip 4″; subcut into 4 rectangles 4″ × 7″ for E pieces
Green/red batik	¾ yard	6 strips 3½″ for outer border
Binding fabric	½ yard	
Backing fabric	3 yards	
Batting	52½″ × 52½″	

Pieces Needed

Unit	Big SIS			Diamond			Little SIS	
FINISHED SIZE	6″ × 6″			3″ × 6″			3″ × 3″	
Pieces Needed	A ▫	B ◺	C ◹	D ◹	Dr ◺	E ◇	F ▫	G ▫
▫ Assorted light golds		16	4	62	64	20	24	46
▨ Assorted dark metallic golds	6	8	4	14	12	6	8	30
▪ Dark red batik				4	4	4	4	20
▪ Dark green batik				4	4	4	4	20
▪ Medium red metallic	2		8			4		
▪ Medium green metallic	2		8			4		

unit assembly

You can either use the foundation template patterns, page 76, to make the units or use the Quilters' TRIMplates and refer to the TRIMplates Piecing section (pages 25–35). The Quilters' TRIMplates are available from C&T Publishing (see Resources, page 78).

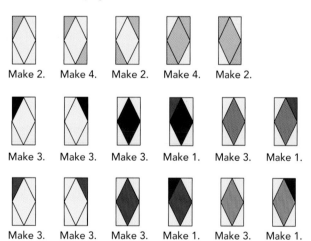

Make 2. Make 4. Make 2. Make 4. Make 2.

Make 3. Make 3. Make 3. Make 1. Make 3. Make 1.

Make 3. Make 3. Make 3. Make 1. Make 3. Make 1.

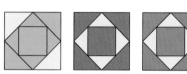

Make 2. Make 2. Make 2.
Big SIS units

Make 4. Make 4. Make 8. Make 3. Make 3. Make 1. Make 1.
Little SIS units

Make 2. Make 2. Make 10. Make 2.
Partial Little SIS units

Using the same sew-and-flip method used to piece the Little SIS units (page 23), make the following units by sewing 1 A or 1 G square on 1 corner of a 6½″ light gold square.

Make 4.   Make 1.   Make 1.

quilt construction

1. Refer to the quilt assembly diagram and arrange the pieced units, the 3½″ × 6½″ light gold rectangles, and the remaining 6½″ light gold squares into rows.

2. Sew the units into rows; press the seams to one side. Sew the rows together; press the seams open.

3. Measure the quilt horizontally. Sew 3 green/red batik strips together end to end, and then cut 2 strips to the measured length. Sew the strips to the top and bottom of the quilt. Press toward the strips.

4. Measure the quilt top vertically, including the borders just added. Sew the remaining green/red batik strips together end to end, and then cut 2 strips to the measured length. Sew the strips to the sides of the quilt. Press.

5. Layer the quilt top, batting, and backing. Baste. Quilt as desired. Add sleeve and binding.

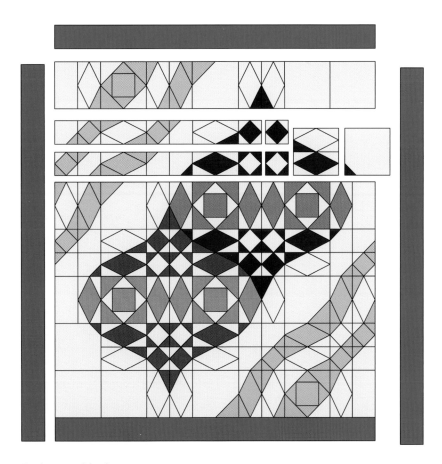

Quilt assembly diagram

Standard grid

Double diamond grid

FOUNDATION-PIECING TEMPLATE PATTERNS

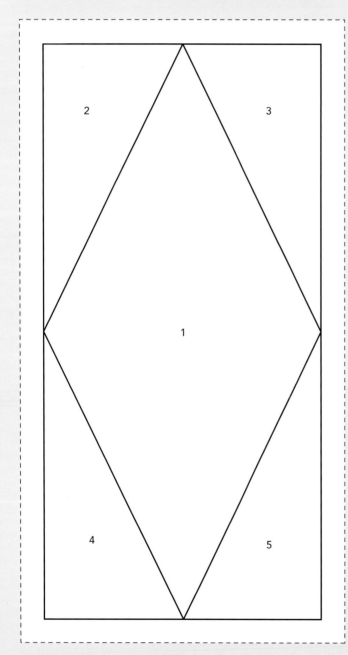

Paper-foundation-piecing pattern for Diamond unit

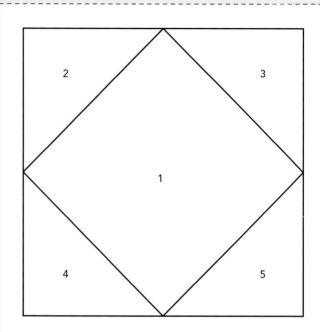

Paper-foundation-piecing pattern for Little SIS unit

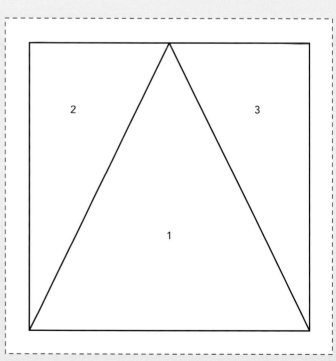

Paper-foundation-piecing pattern for TIS unit

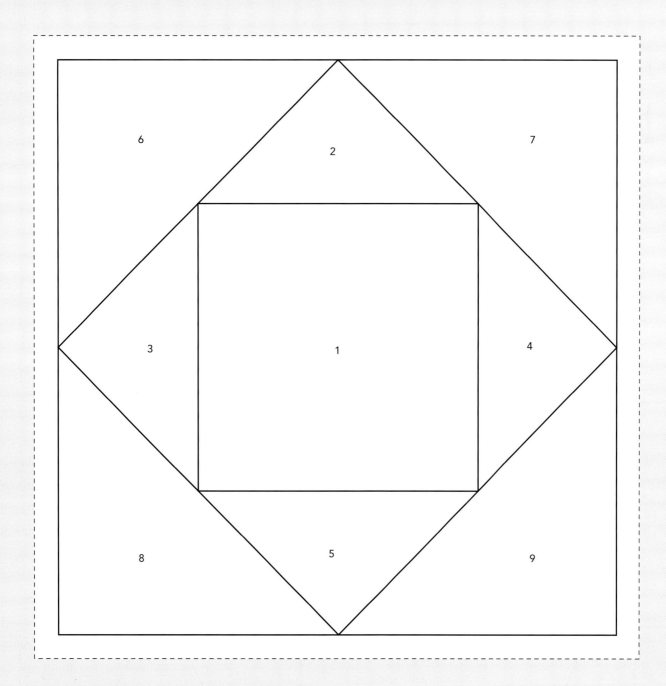

Paper-foundation-piecing pattern for Big SIS unit

tip For ease of foundation piecing,
cut the individual pieces ³⁄₈″
larger all around than the given pattern
shape. For general instructions on paper
piecing, see the *Carol Doak Teaches You to
Paper Piece* DVD (see Resources, page 78).

resources

For a list of other fine books from C&T Publishing, ask for a free catalog:

C&T PUBLISHING, INC.

P.O. Box 1456

Lafayette, CA 94549

(800) 284-1114

Email: ctinfo@ctpub.com

Website: www.ctpub.com

C&T Publishing's professional photography services are now available to the public. Visit us at www.ctmediaservices.com.

For quilting supplies:

COTTON PATCH

1025 Brown Ave.

Lafayette, CA 94549

Store: (925) 284-1177

Mail order: (925) 283-7883

Email: CottonPa@aol.com

Website: www.quiltusa.com

Note: Fabrics used in the quilts shown may not be currently available, as fabric manufacturers keep most fabrics in print for only a short time.

Recommended Products

Quilters' TRIMplates,
C&T Publishing

Piecing Tips and Tricks Tool,
C&T Publishing

All-in-One Quilter's Reference Tool,
C&T Publishing

Recommended Videos

Carol Doak Teaches You to Paper Piece,
C&T Publishing

Recommended Books

Fabric of Faith: A Guide to The Prayer Quilt Ministry by Kimberly Winston; Morehouse Publishing, 2006.

Mastering Precision Piecing by Sally Collins,
C&T Publishing

A Garden Party of Quilts by Joen Wolfrom,
C&T Publishing

Shoreline Quilts by Cyndy Lyle Rymer,
C&T Publishing

about the author

Wendy Mathson has been making and designing quilts since 1981, beginning with a baby quilt made in anticipation of the birth of her first child. Since then she has been involved in the quilting community in the San Diego area, first as a guild member, later as a teacher, and more recently as a guild lecturer. In 1992, she was part of a quilting circle at her church that began making prayer quilts. A few years later, Wendy organized Prayers & Squares, The Prayer Quilt Ministry. This interfaith nonprofit organization now has over 800 chapters worldwide. She began designing and teaching simple strip-pieced patterns to be used for prayer quilts. Wendy loves coming up with ideas for improved piecing techniques and has invented a system of cut-after-you-sew tools called Quilters' TRIMplates.

Photo by Brooke A. Farrington, Lifetouch Portrait Studios Inc.

Wendy now works as a freelance book editor/illustrator and teaches quilting classes for a local community college. She and her husband, Dan, have lived in the San Diego area for over 25 years and are the parents of two grown children, Scott and Michelle.

You can contact Wendy at wmathson@cox.net or P.O. Box 156, Poway, CA 92074.

Great Titles
from 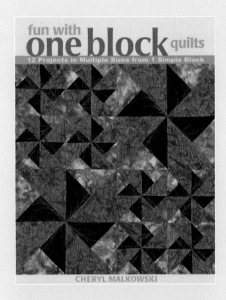 C&T PUBLISHING

fun with
one block quilts
12 Projects in Multiple Sizes from 1 Simple Block

CHERYL MALKOWSKI

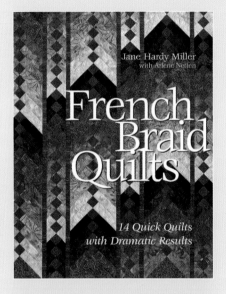

Jane Hardy Miller
with Arlene Netten

French Braid Quilts

*14 Quick Quilts
with Dramatic Results*

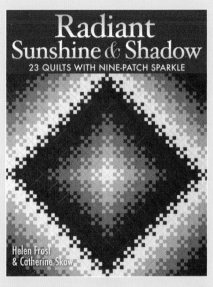

Radiant
Sunshine & Shadow
23 QUILTS WITH NINE-PATCH SPARKLE

Helen Frost
& Catherine Skow

One-Block Wonders
encore!
New Shapes, Multiple Fabrics, Out-of-this-World Quilts

MAXINE ROSENTHAL & JOY PELZMANN

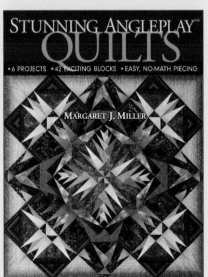

STUNNING ANGLEPLAY™
QUILTS
• 6 PROJECTS • 42 EXCITING BLOCKS • EASY, NO-MATH PIECING

MARGARET J. MILLER

PEGGY J. BARKLE
blendable curves
STACK, SLICE & SEW UNIQUE QUILTS IN A WEEKEND